Editor   April McCroskie

Language Consultant   Prue Goodwin

Dr Gerald Legg holds a doctorate in zoology from Manchester University. His current position is biologist at the Booth Museum of Natural History in Brighton.

Carolyn Scrace is a graduate of Brighton College of Art, specialising in design and illustration. She has worked in animation, advertising and children's fiction. She is a major contributor to the popular *Worldwise* series.

Prue Goodwin is a lecturer in Language in Education, and director of INSET at the *Reading and Language Information Centre* at the University of Reading.

David Salariya was born in Dundee, Scotland, where he studied illustration and printmaking, concentrating on book design in his postgraduate year. He has designed and created many new series of children's books for publishers in the U.K. and overseas.

The Cataloging-In-Publication Data is available from the Library of Congress

ISBN 0-531-14492-5

An SBC Book
Conceived, edited and designed by
The Salariya Book Company
25 Marlborough Place Brighton BN1 1UB
© The Salariya Book Company Ltd MCMXCVII

First published in Great Britain by
Franklin Watts
96 Leonard Street
London
EC2A 4RH

First American edition 1998 by
Franklin Watts
A Division of Grolier Publishing
Sherman Turnpike
Danbury, CT 06816

Printed in Belgium

lifecycles

From Seed to Sunflower

Written by Dr Gerald Legg
Illustrated by Carolyn Scrace

Created & Designed by David Salariya

A FRANKLIN WATTS
LIBRARY EDITION

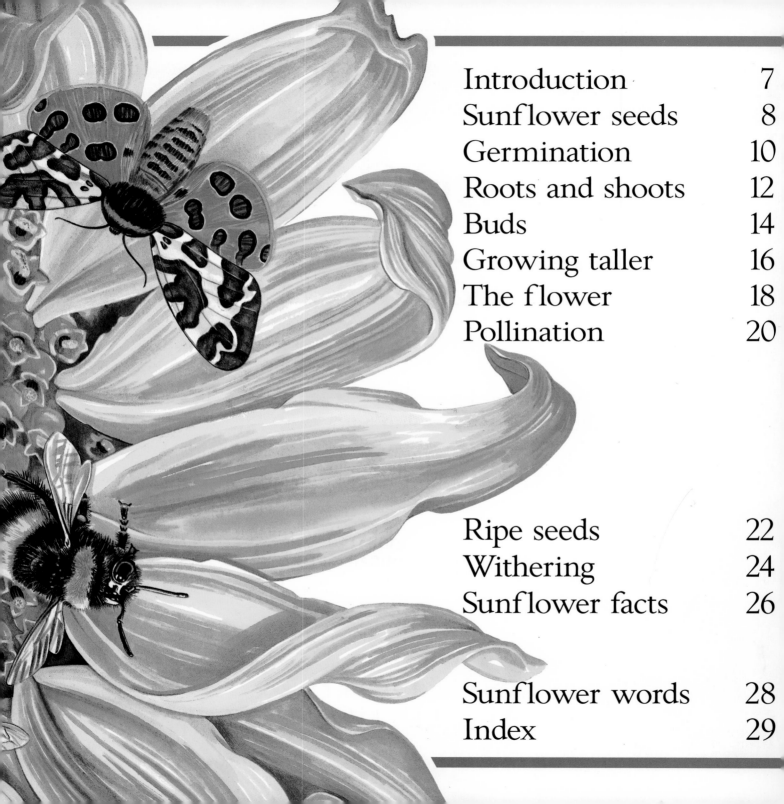

Plants use energy from the sun to make food. Minerals in the soil also help plants to grow. In this book you can see how a tiny seed grows into a beautiful sunflower.

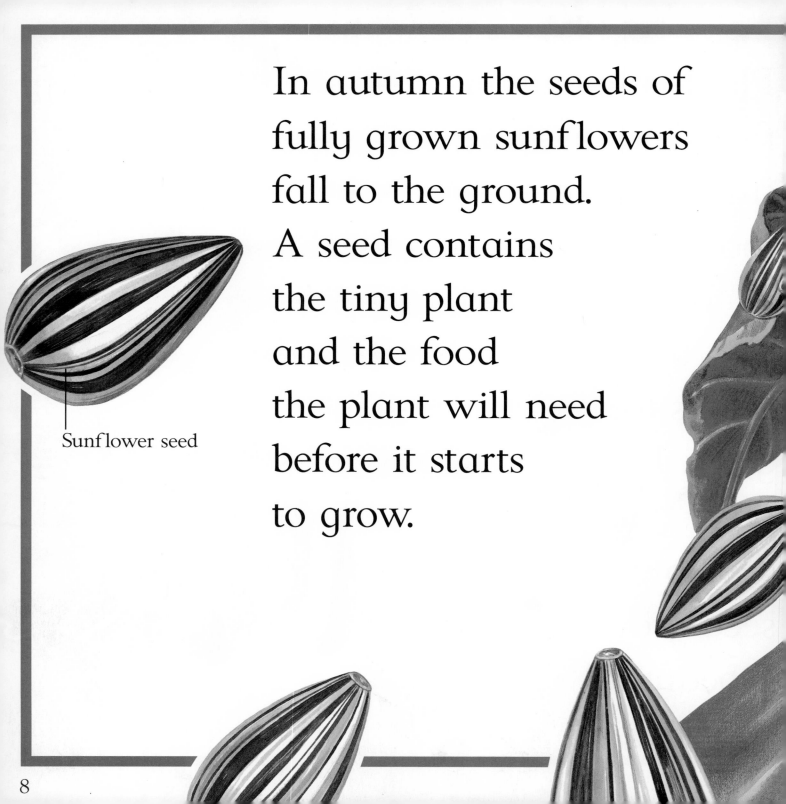

In autumn the seeds of
fully grown sunflowers
fall to the ground.
A seed contains
the tiny plant
and the food
the plant will need
before it starts
to grow.

Sunflower seed

The seeds are buried in the soil.
The soil contains minerals.
Minerals are special foods
that help the plant to grow.
In spring the warm sun and rain
make the seeds begin to grow.
This is called germination.

The seed lies
buried in the soil
all through
the winter.

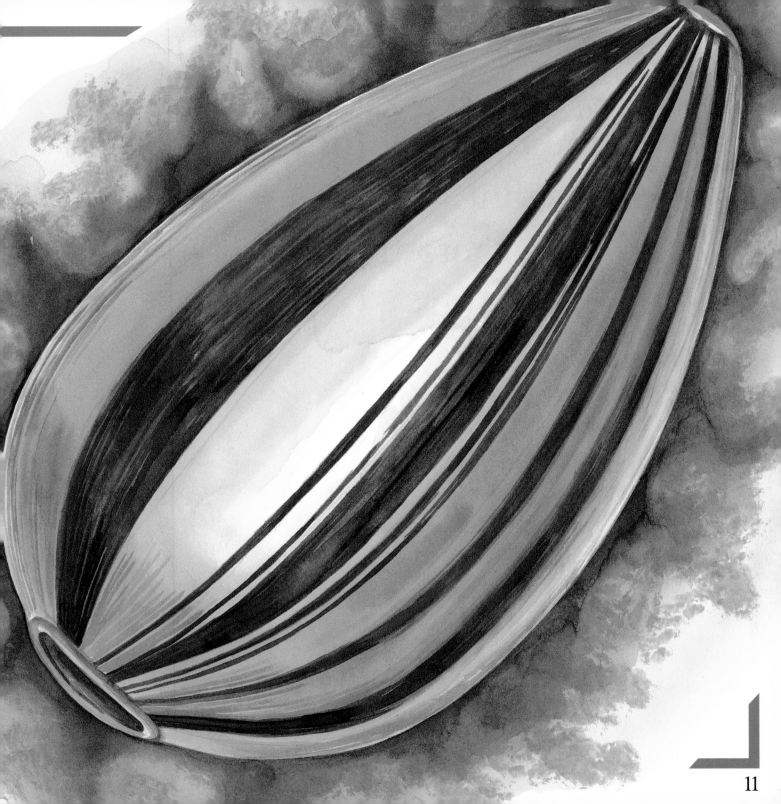

The tough seed coat splits.
Then the first root grows out.
It knows that it must
grow down into the soil.
Soon afterwards
a shoot will sprout,
pushing the seed coat
out of the soil.
It knows it must
grow up
into the air.

Root ———————————

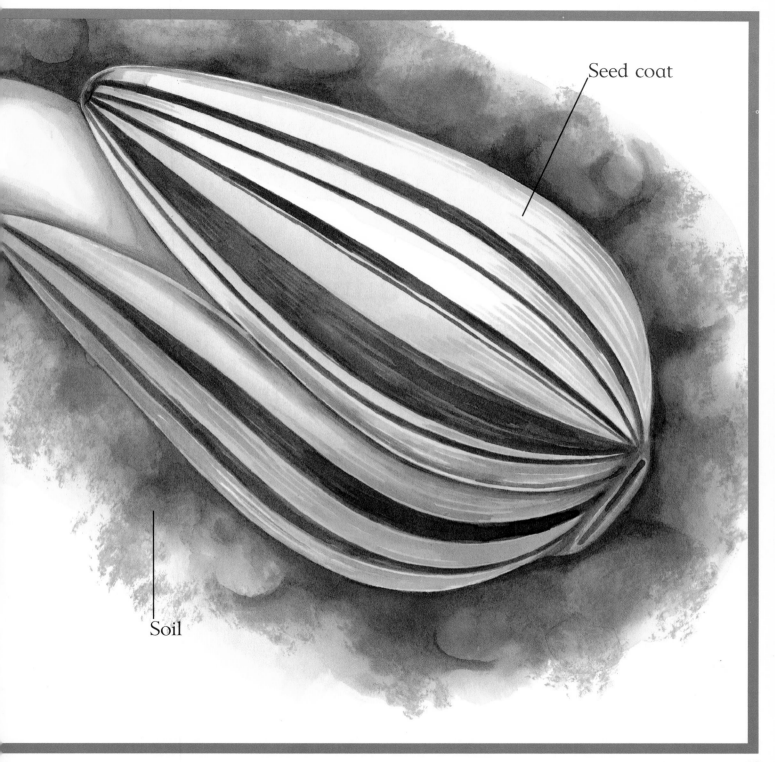

Seed coat

Soil

13

Food stored inside the seed
helps the plant to grow.
Smaller roots begin to sprout
from the larger root.
The roots collect minerals
and water from the soil
to feed the growing plant.
A bud hidden between the
seed leaves pushes away
the split seed coat.

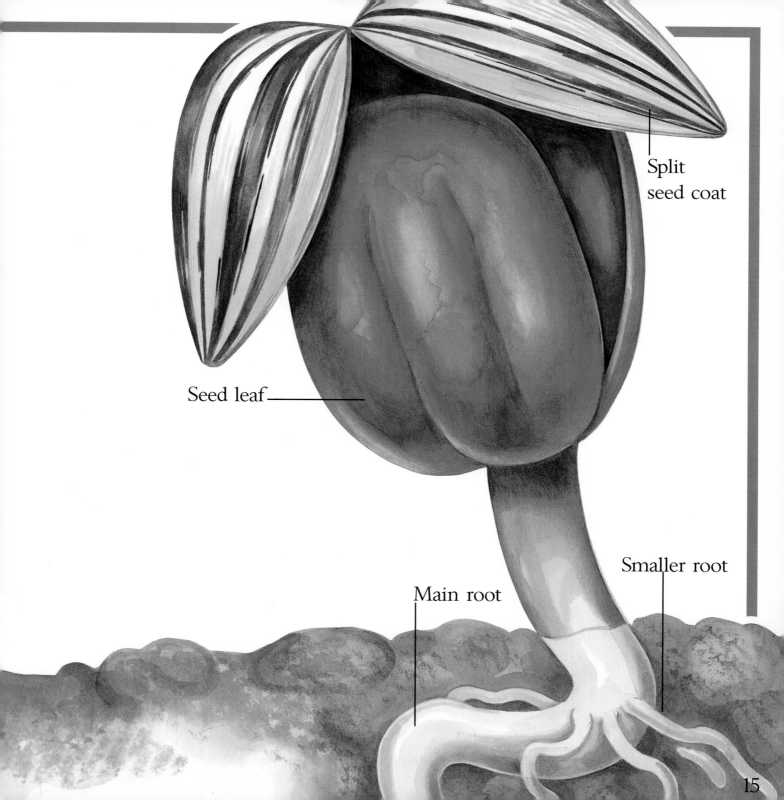

Split
seed coat

Seed leaf

Smaller root

Main root

15

Lady bug

The young sunflower grows taller and more leaves sprout. The leaves use air, water, and sunlight to make food. Flower buds form and the roots grow longer. The roots take in water from the soil and help to hold the sunflower steady.

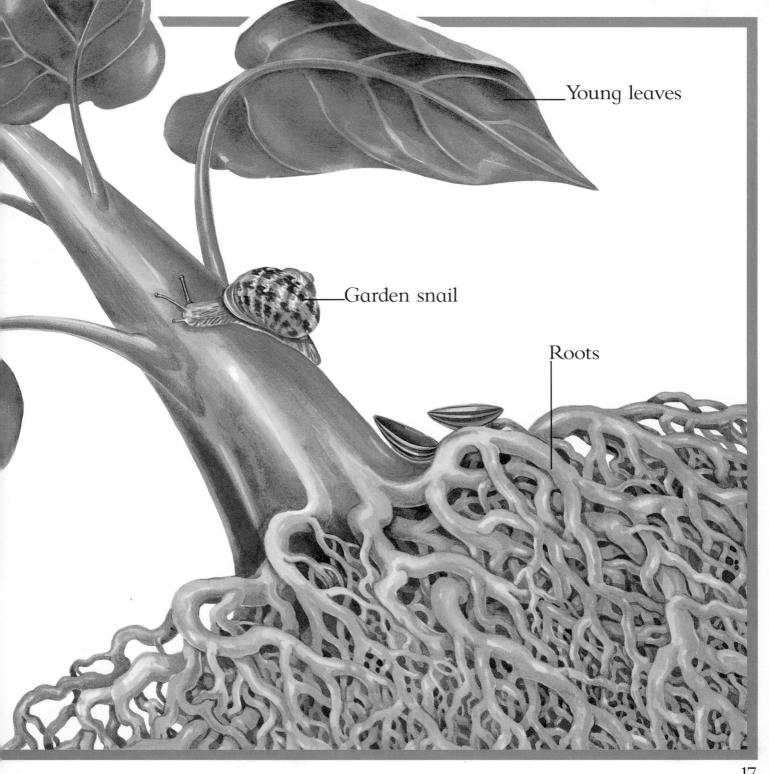

Young leaves

Garden snail

Roots

The flower bud grows
at the top of the stem.
Later it will open up
into a large flower head.
Each flower head is
made of lots of tiny flowers
packed together.
These tiny flowers
produce seeds.

Lady bug

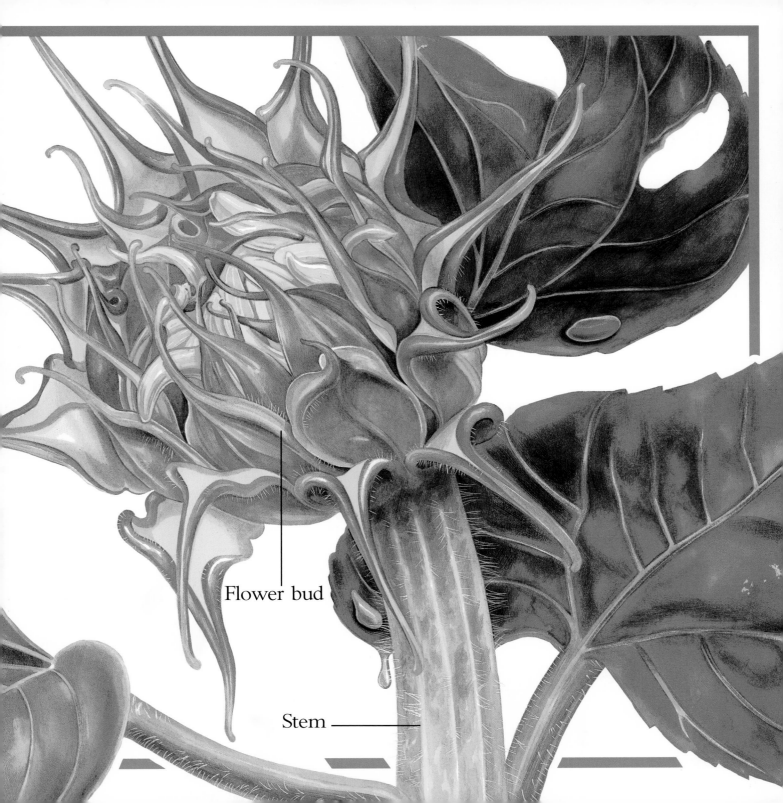

Flower bud

Stem

Insects are attracted to flowers
because flowers make
sweet nectar and pollen.
Insects drink nectar and,
as they fly between the plants,
they also carry
the sticky pollen
on the plants
from flower to flower.
It is the pollen that makes
plants produce new seeds.
This is called pollination.

The tiny seeds ripen.
Birds peck the seeds
in the flower heads.
Some seeds are eaten
and some are blown
away by the wind.
Some are caught in animal fur
and fall to the ground later.
Seeds can be carried far away
from the mother plant.

In autumn the sunflower withers and dies. The seeds that have not been eaten or carried away fall to the ground. These seeds will be ready to grow next spring.

The seeds fall to the ground.

Withered flower head

Sunflower facts

Sunflower seeds are around .4 inches long.

The sunflower is a tall plant that can grow to 11.5 feet high.

The main root of the sunflower can grow 10 feet down into the ground.

The sunflower head can grow to around 16 inches across.

Some gardeners grow ornamental sunflowers with red, striped petals.

The main leaves of the sunflower are heart-shaped. They are around 1 foot across and 8 inches long.

The sunflower turns its head towards the sun and follows it across the sky. In some countries it is called a sun-seeker.

Sunflowers were grown originally by Native Americans, from Southern Canada to Mexico.

The growth of a sunflower
In spring the seed-coat splits and the root and shoot sprout. The root and the shoot use minerals from the soil to grow. The plant then buds and a sunflower grows. In autumn the sunflower withers and the seeds fall to the ground.

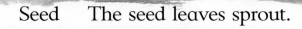

Seed　　The seed leaves sprout.　　5 weeks　　9 week

Around 200 years ago farmers started to grow sunflowers so that the seeds could be crushed to make sunflower oil.

Sunflowers are mainly grown in America, but they are also grown in Europe.

Oil from the seeds is used for cooking. The seeds themselves can be eaten, too.

The remains of the crushed seeds can be used as animal feed.

Budding   12 weeks   Flowering   Fully grown   Withering   Falling seeds

Sunflower words

Bud
The top of a shoot or branch. New leaves and flowers grow inside the bud.

Extinct
A plant or animal that has died out forever.

Germination
The stage in the life cycle of a plant when the seeds first begin to grow.

Minerals
Special food in the soil. Plants need minerals to help them grow.

Nectar
Sweet, sugary liquid made by flowers to attract insects.

Pollen
The fine dust of a male flower. Insects and wind transfer pollen to the female plant. When this happens seeds are made.

Pollination
The movement of pollen from one flower to another.

Root
The part of a plant that grows down into the soil.

Seed
The part of the plant that contains the young plant. When it grows the young plant appears.

Seed coat
The tough outer layer of a seed.

Seed leaves
The very first leaves that a plant grows when it grows from the seed.

Shoot
The young branch or stem of a plant.

Stem
The part of the plant that grows up into the air. Flowers and leaves grow from the stem.

Wither
To dry up.

Index